The Scale Of...

BUILDINGS & STRUCTURES

By Joanna Brundle

BookLife
PUBLISHING

©2019
BookLife Publishing Ltd.
King's Lynn
Norfolk PE30 4LS

Printed in Malaysia.

A catalogue record for this book is available from the British Library.

ISBN: 978-1-78637-879-8

Written by:
Joanna Brundle

Edited by:
Emilie Dufresne

Designed by:
Jasmine Pointer

Photocredits

All images courtesy of Shutterstock.com. With thanks to Getty Images, Thinkstock Photo and iStockphoto.

Front Cover – Boyko.Pictures, gst. 2–3 – Malika Keehl. 4–5 – KittyVector. 6–7 – Naty_Lee, NotionPic, Tako design. 8–9 – Tako design, larry laurence marcelo, twins_nika, rorrak. 10–11 – Champ008, MatoomMi, BILEY-16. 12–13 – Walking-onstreet, vberla. 14–15 – Merfin. 16–17 – Red monkey, ONYXprj, studioworkstock, Zarica. 18–19 – Fay Francevna, Rattanamanee Patpong. 20–21 – ProStockStudio. .

CONTENTS

Words that look like this can be found in the glossary on page 24.

INTRODUCTION

The scale of things means how one thing compares in size to another. In this book, we will be comparing famous buildings and structures by finding out how tall they are.

We will be measuring the heights of different buildings in metres. A door in your house or school is around two metres high. This should help you imagine how tall these buildings are.

Some famous buildings and structures are less than one hundred metres tall. Others are many hundreds of metres tall. It is easy to see why the tall buildings are called skyscrapers. Let's start comparing.

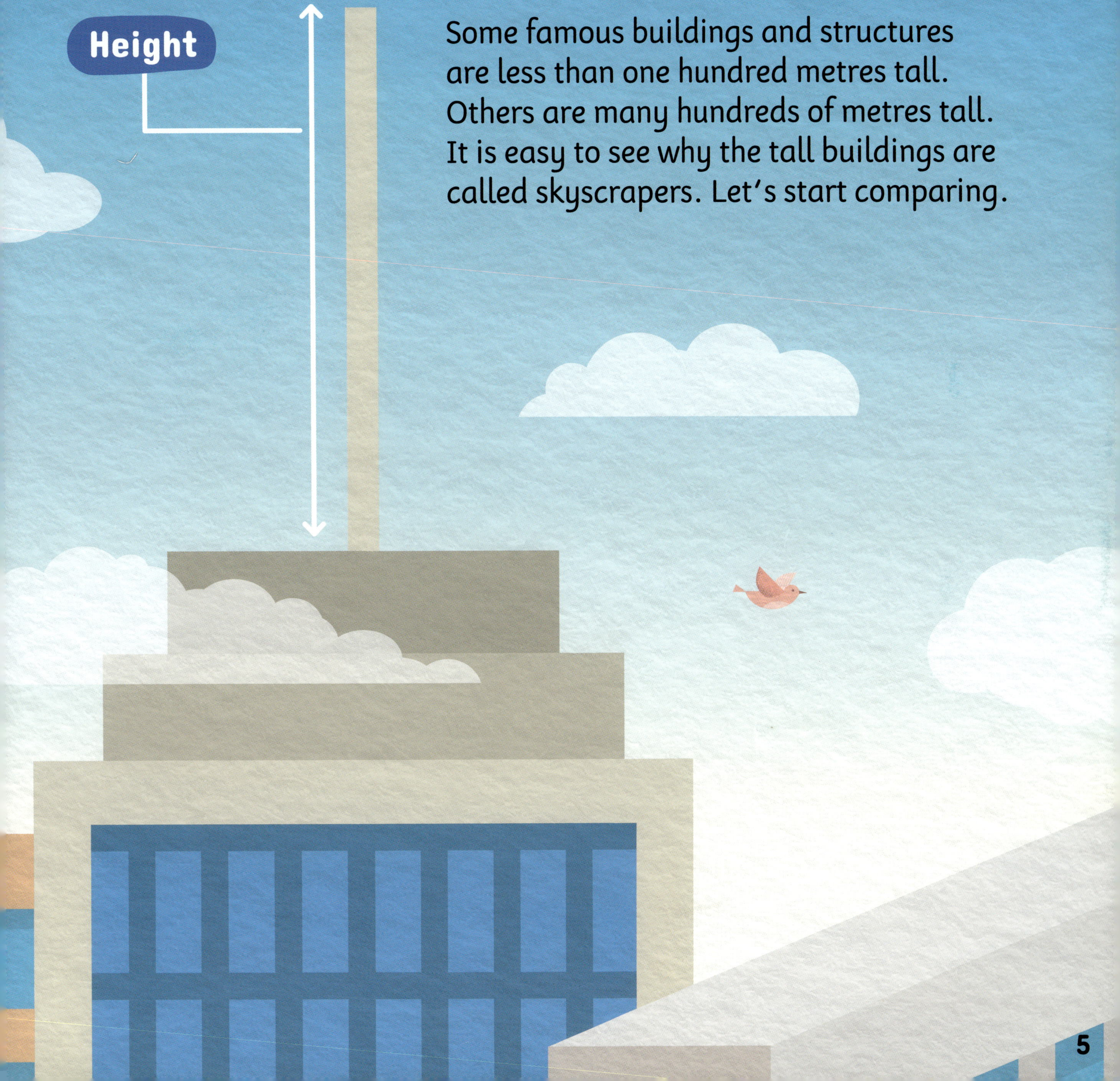

THE COLOSSEUM AND THE LEANING TOWER OF PISA

The Colosseum is the largest amphitheatre in the world. Inside, gladiators used to fight one another in front of huge crowds. The Colosseum is in Rome, Italy.

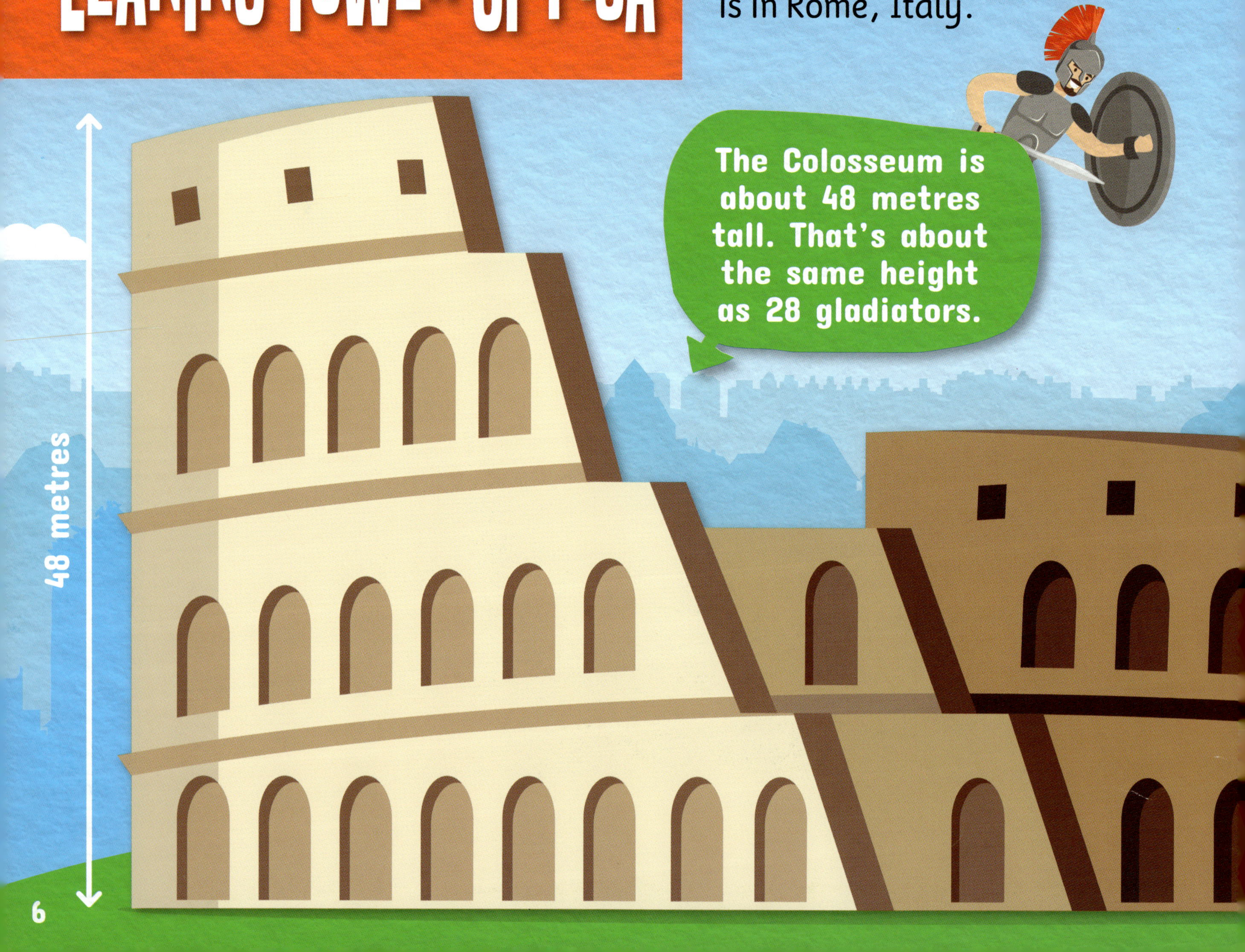

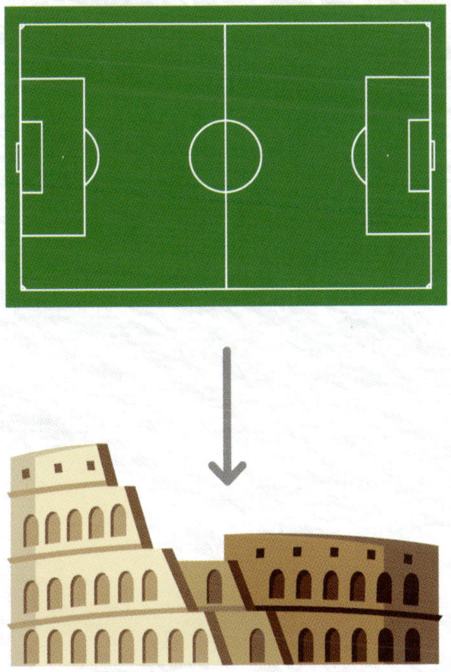

The Leaning Tower of Pisa is about as tall as the Colosseum with two double decker buses piled on top.

A football pitch could easily fit inside the Colosseum. There was room for around 50,000 spectators.

THE LEANING TOWER OF PISA AND THE STATUE OF LIBERTY

There are over 250 steps to reach the top of the Leaning Tower of Pisa.

The Leaning Tower of Pisa is around 57 metres tall at its highest point. Although it was built standing straight, the tower started leaning because it was built on soft soil.

The Statue of Liberty is 93 metres tall. That's as high as the Leaning Tower of Pisa with eight double decker buses piled on top.

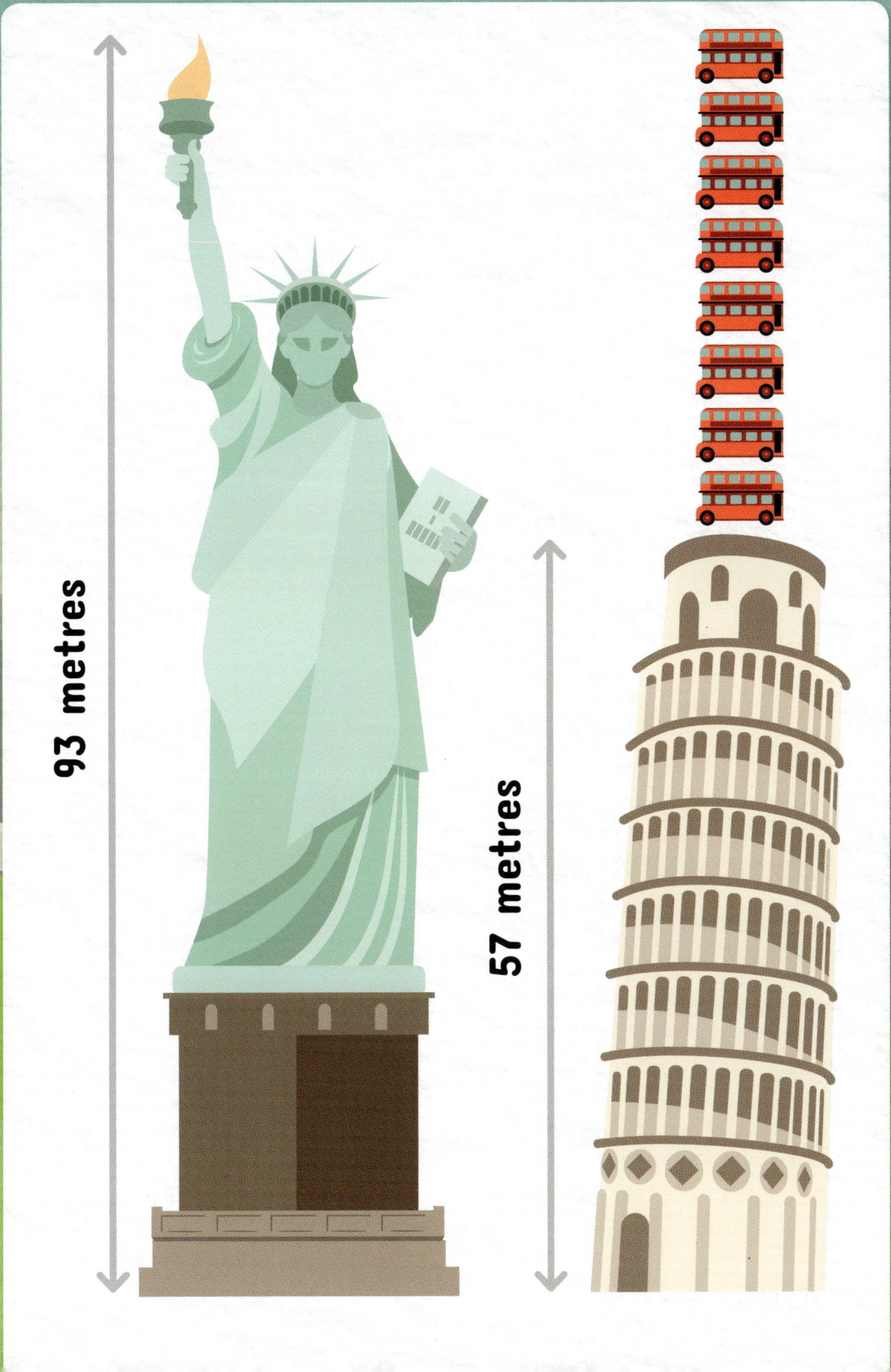

The difference in height is also about the same as 101 large pizzas, side by side.

THE STATUE OF LIBERTY AND THE LONDON EYE

Lady Liberty's sandals are nearly eight metres long. Her shoe size would be 922.

The Statue of Liberty stands on Liberty Island in New York Harbour in the US. The statue is of Lady Liberty – a symbol of freedom. She carries a torch. The flame is covered in gold leaf.

The London Eye is 135 metres tall. That's about the same height as the Statue of Liberty with ten double decker buses piled on top.

THE LONDON EYE AND GOLDEN GATE BRIDGE

The London Eye is nearly 200 times larger than the wheel of an adult's bicycle.

The London Eye is a giant turning <u>observation wheel</u> in the UK. There are 32 pods on the wheel. <u>Passengers</u> stand in the pods and can view London in all directions for up to 40 kilometres.

The towers of the Golden Gate Bridge rise 227 metres above the water. That's nearly as high as the London Eye and the Statue of Liberty joined together.

GOLDEN GATE BRIDGE AND THE EIFFEL TOWER

The Golden Gate Bridge is in San Francisco, US. It crosses a stretch of water called the Golden Gate.

Over 100,000 vehicles cross the bridge every day.

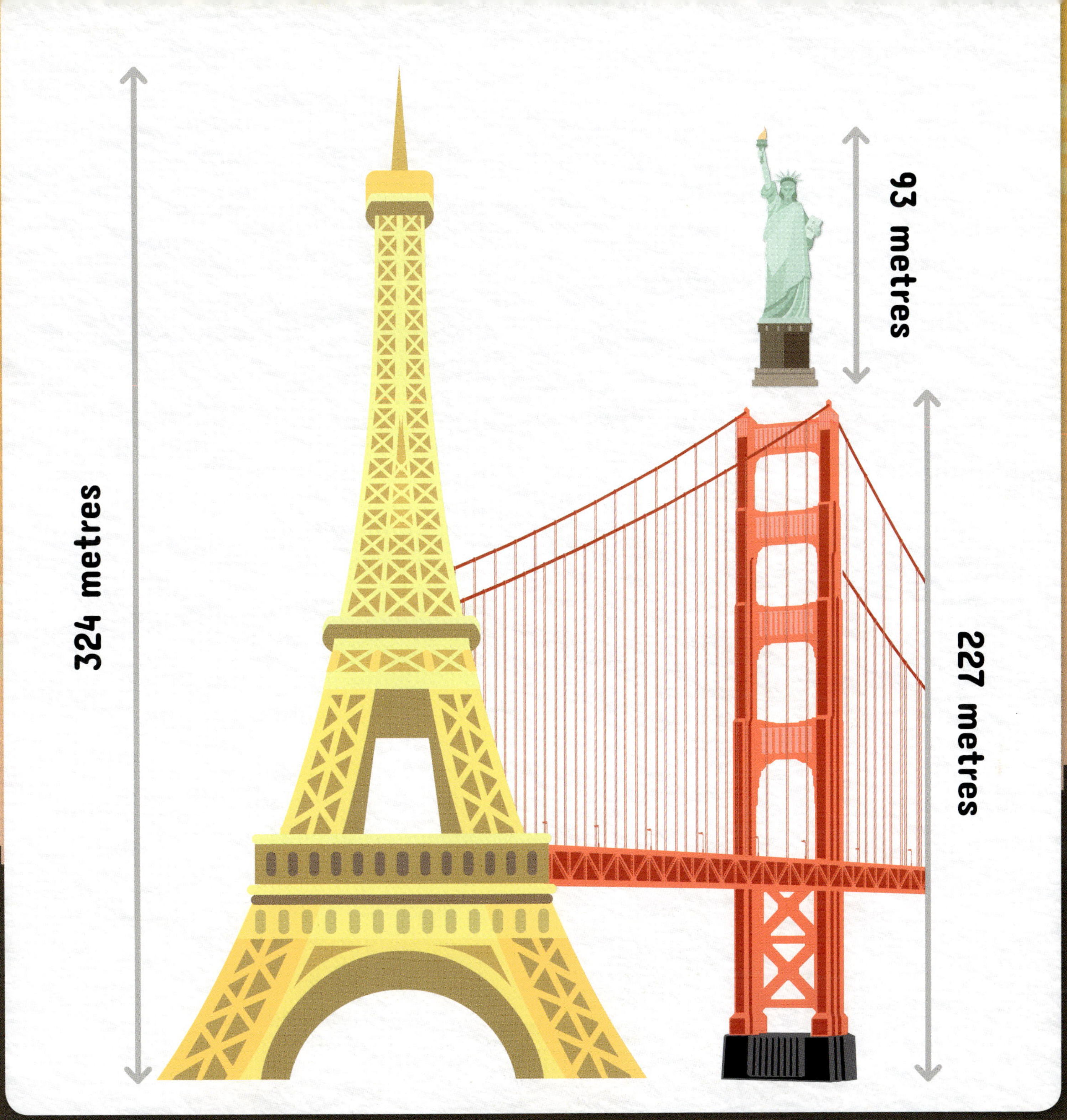

The Eiffel Tower is 324 metres tall from the base to the tip. That's taller than the Golden Gate Bridge and the Statue of Liberty joined together.

THE EIFFEL TOWER AND THE EMPIRE STATE BUILDING

The Eiffel Tower is an iron lattice tower in Paris, France. Visitors can climb around 674 steps to reach the second floor. At night, the tower is lit up by **20,000** light bulbs.

Climbing 674 steps is like climbing the staircase in a house about 52 times.

The Empire State Building is 443 metres tall. That's taller than the Eiffel Tower with two Leaning Towers of Pisa stacked on top.

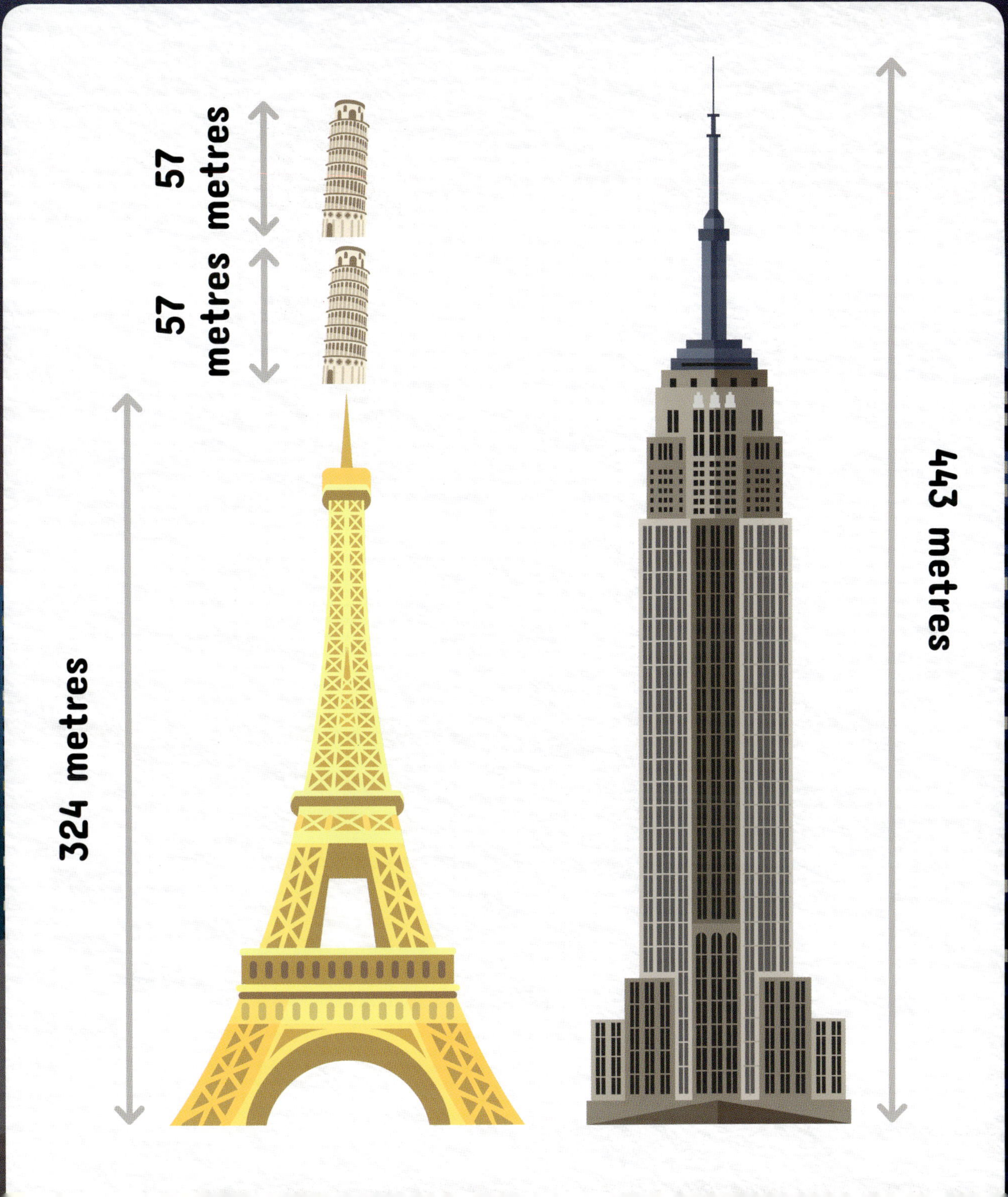

THE EMPIRE STATE BUILDING AND SHANGHAI TOWER

The Empire State Building is in New York City, US. It has 103 floors, with 1,860 steps up to the 102nd floor. Visitors can look out from the 102nd floor and the 86th floor.

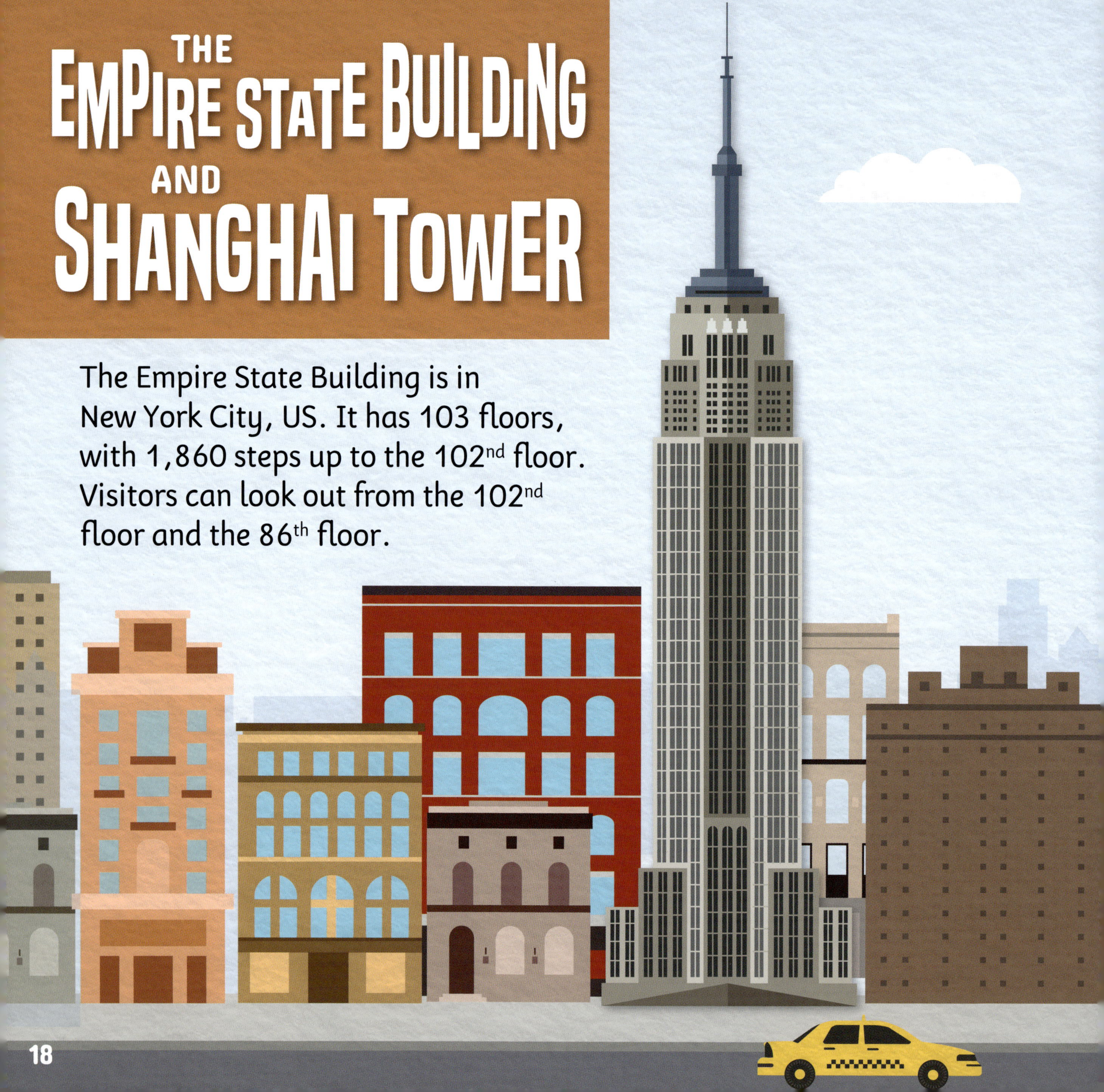

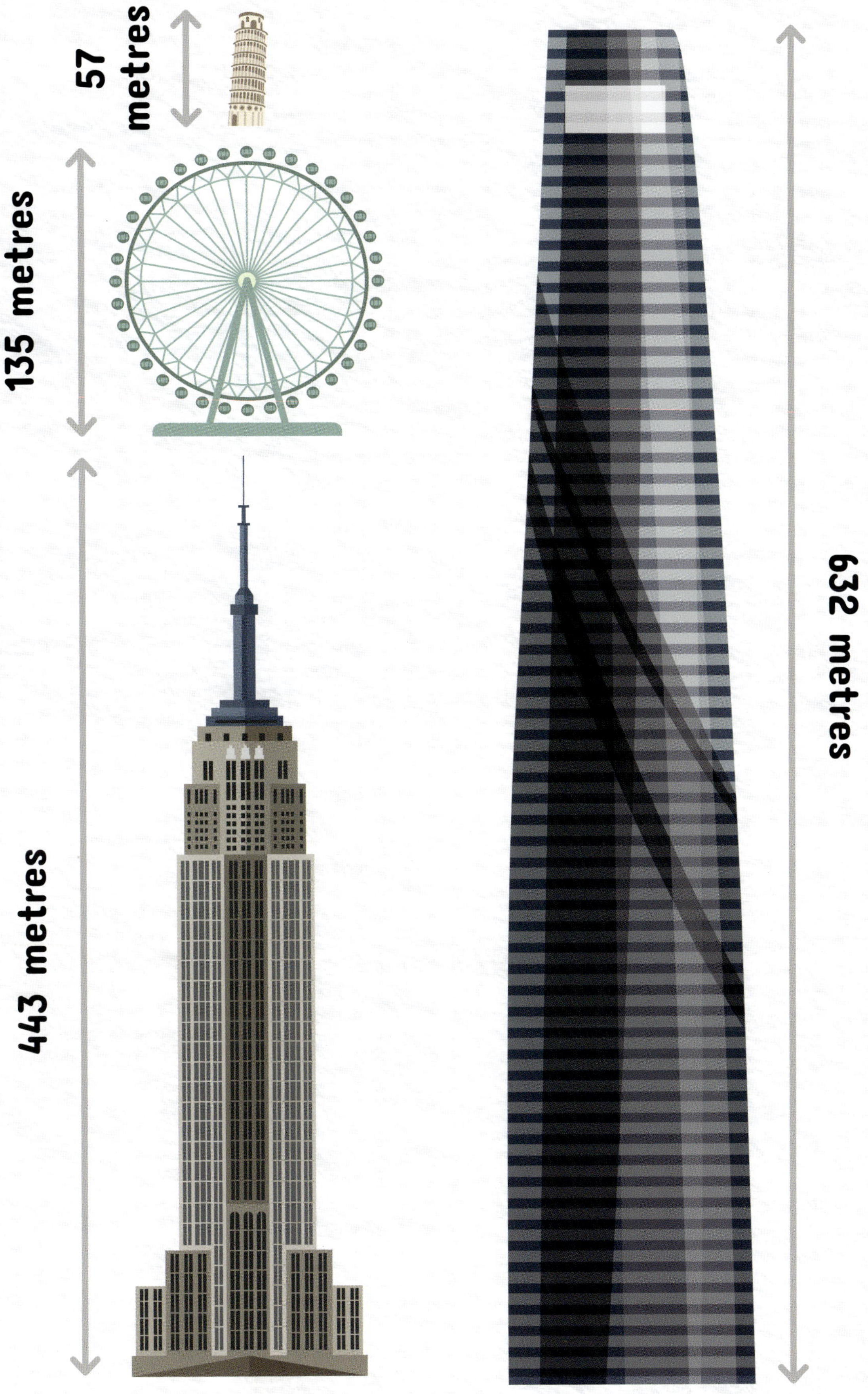

Shanghai Tower in China is 632 metres tall. That's almost as tall as the Empire State Building, the London Eye and the Leaning Tower of Pisa piled up on top of each other.

SHANGHAI TOWER AND BURJ KHALIFA

Shanghai Tower has over 125 floors above ground. A viewing deck on the 118th floor gives great views of the city. The tower has one of the fastest lifts in the world.

The Burj Khalifa in Dubai is 828 metres tall. That's taller than Shanghai Tower, the London Eye and the Leaning Tower of Pisa stacked on top of each other.

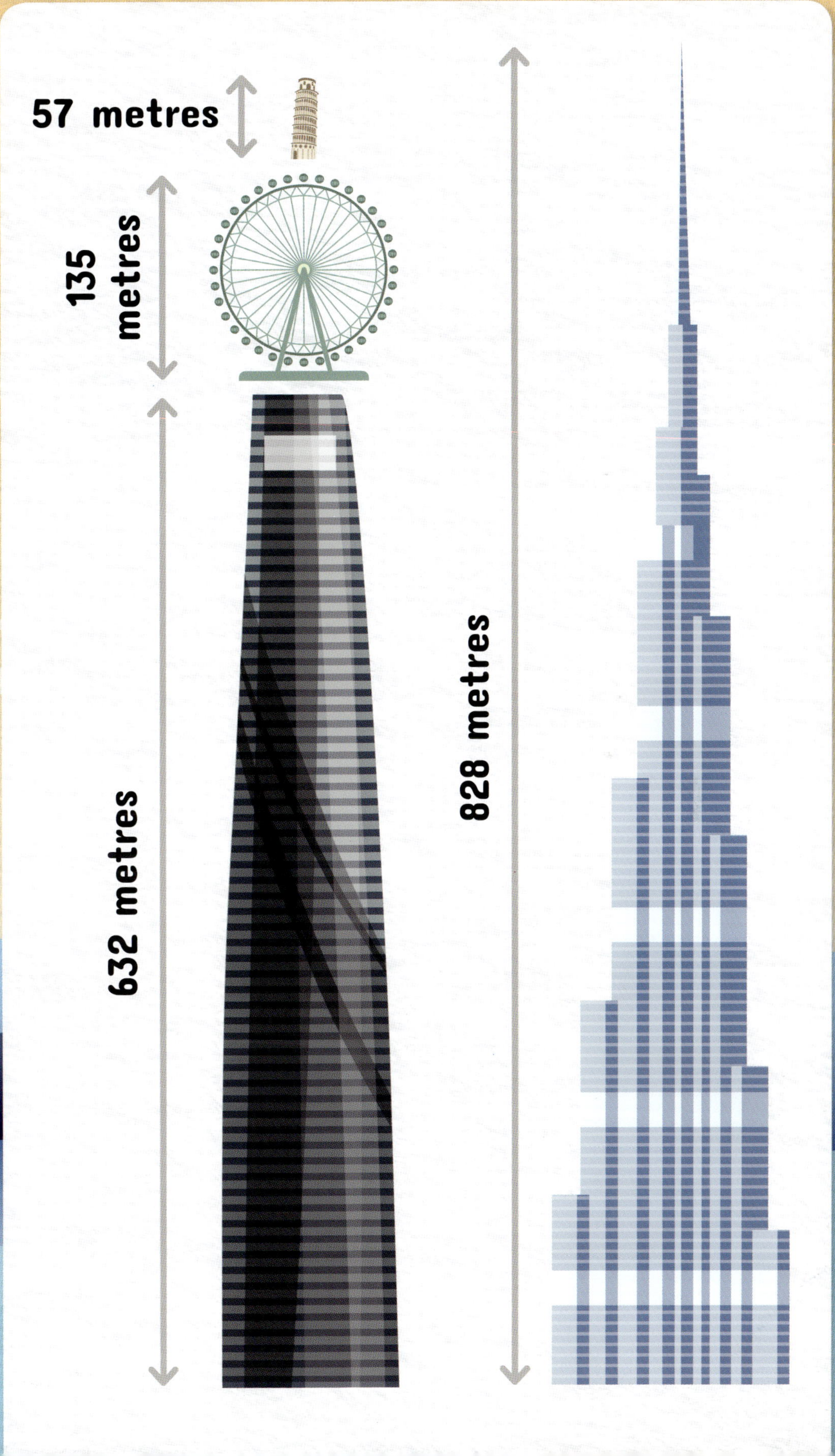

BURJ KHALIFA

The Burj Khalifa has more than 160 floors. Inside, there are restaurants, offices, apartments and a hotel. Its shape is based on a flower called the spider lily.

The Burj Khalifa was the tallest skyscraper in the world when it opened in 2010. Only two-thirds of the Burj Khalifa can be used by humans. The rest is just for show and height.

Taller and taller structures keep being built all the time.

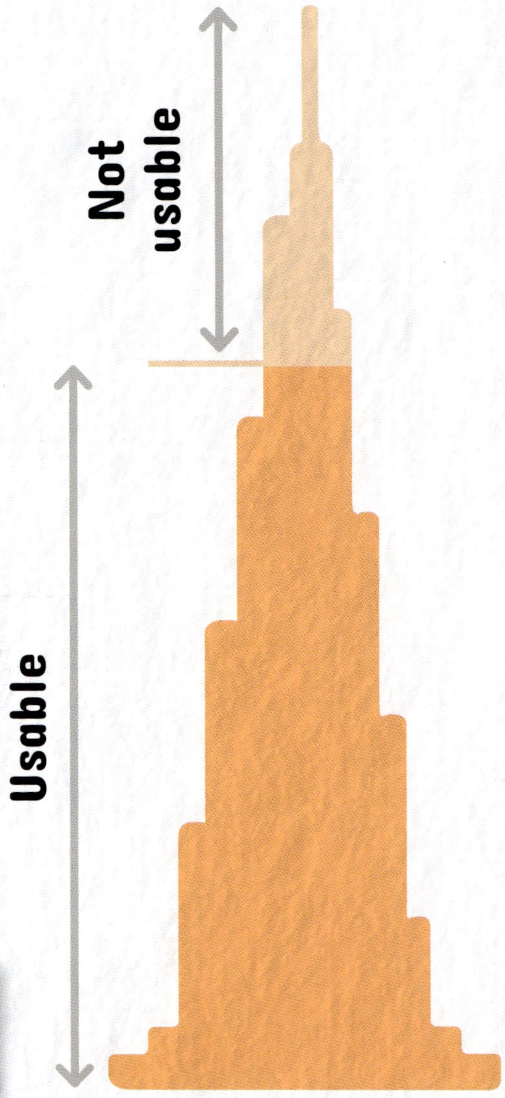

GLOSSARY

amphitheatre an open, round theatre with layers of seats for spectators

apartments small parts of a building which are used for living in, such as rooms or flats

gladiators men trained to fight at ancient Roman shows

gold leaf gold that has been beaten into a very thin sheet that can put onto things such as statues

lattice tower a tower made up of strips of wood or metal which form a criss-cross pattern

lifts platforms or compartments used to raise and lower people to different levels in a building

observation wheel a wheel that people can use to see for long distances

passengers people who are carried in or on something that is moving

spectators the people who are watching a sport or event

symbol a thing that is used as a sign of something else

viewing deck an area of a high building which allows people to look at the view

INDEX